The Twit

The Saxon and Norman lanes of Lewes

Kim Clark

Cover illustration: Keere Street © Marietta van Dyck
Title page illustration: Town Fox © Peter Messer

Published by Pomegranate Press,
Dolphin House, 51 St Nicholas Lane, Lewes, Sussex BN7 2JZ
pomegranatepress@aol.com
www.pomegranate-press.co.uk

ISBN: 978–1–907242–30–4

British Library Cataloguing-in-Publication Data.
A catalogue record for this book is available from the British Library

Printed and bound by 4Edge, 7A Eldon Way, Hockley, Essex SS4 2DA

Contents

PLAN

of the BOROUGH of LEWES, in the

COUNTY of SUSSEX,

Taken from an Actual Survey; and exhibiting all Ancient Boundaries
as attentively Perambulated by the Constables and having on One Body,

ON THE 15th DAY of OCTr IN THE YEAR 1799;

Executed by Order of the present Chief Officers,

WILLIAM LEE and JOHN BAKER,

To the End that the same may be
preserved to the latest Posterity.

THE LORDS of the BOROUGH

His Grace The Duke of Norfolk,
The Earl of Abergavenny,
and His Grace The Duke of Dorset.

PADDOCK belonging to Henry SHELLEY
Esqr.

Scale of 10 Chains, or One Furlong.

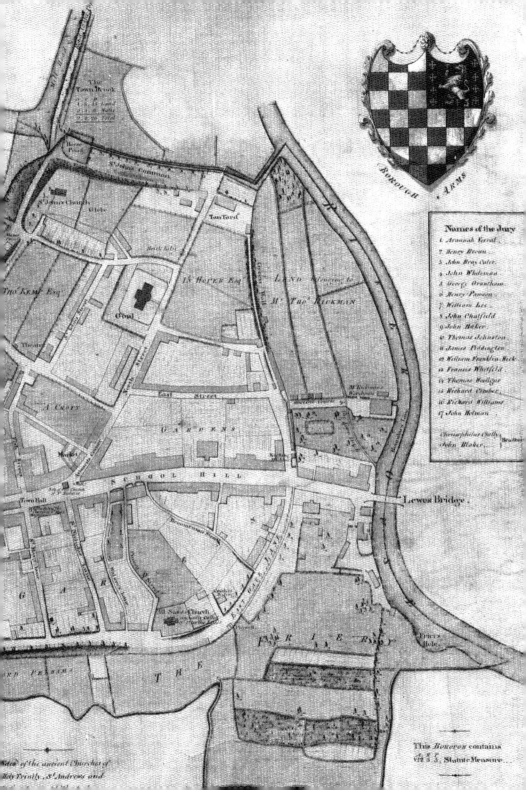

BOROUGH ARMS

The Town Brook

Horse Pond

St John's Common

St John's Church Glebe

Tan Yard

Brick Kiln

IN HOPER Esq

LAND belonging to Mr Thos HICKMAN

Thos KEMP Esq

Gaol

Theatre

A CROSS

East Street

GARDENS

Mr Richmans Warehouse

Auction Court

Market

SCHOOL HILL

Town Hall

Lewes Bridge

GARDENS

All Saints Church

Cockpit

THE OUSE RIVER

Pinwell Hole

This Borough contains
vii 3 5 Statute Measure

Site of the ancient Churches of
Holy Trinity, St Andrews and

Names of the Jury
1. Araanah Verral
2. Henry Brown
3. John Bray Cater
4. John Whiteman
5. George Grantham
6. Henry Parsen
7. William Lee
8. John Chatfield
9. John Baker
10. Thomas Johnston
11. James Piddington
12. William Franklin Nick
13. Francis Whitfield
14. Thomas Hodgur
15. Richard Comber
16. Richard Williams
17. John Holman

Christophilus Chilly   Bendtor
John Blaker

Acknowledgements

I am extremely grateful to the following. Dr Colin Brent and Dr Michael Holmes read the manuscript and made constructive suggestions. I also relied enormously on their original research. Marietta Van Dyck drew all the figures and allowed us to reproduce many of her beautiful prints. Peter Messer gave permission to include several of his paintings, which I first admired in his book *On The Way To Work*.

This book has been published by the Friends of Lewes, and many members have contributed to it. We owe much to the enthusiasm of our chairman, Robert Cheesman. Neil Merchant took all the photographs. Roger Beasley shared his research on the Magic Circle and found photographs of F. Frankfort Moore's garden at Castlegate House. Several members of the Executive Committee read the early draft and made suggestions on how it might be improved: Micheal Turner, Mike Stepney and Jon Gunson were particularly helpful. Marcus Taylor was an extremely vigilant proof reader, continuing to find typing errors when I was certain they had all been spotted. It was Anthony Dicks' idea that we should produce a new book on the Lewes Twittens, and of course I referred often to the original work by John Houghton. David Arscott put everything together.

Finally I must thank my husband Terry for putting up with me and straightening out the many problems with the computer.

Foreword

In 1991 the Friends of Lewes published a short book, *Lewes Twittens,* which was written by John Houghton and illustrated with sketches by another member, Arthur Stronell. As Peter Linklater, the chairman of the Friends at the time, said in his introduction 'the purpose of this book is to spotlight their existence and to alert everybody to their vulnerability'. The book therefore highlighted the principal concerns about the erosion of the unique character of the twittens and made suggestions regarding their conservation in the future.

In the twenty years since *Lewes Twittens* was published there have been a few successes – parking in Keere Street has been forbidden, except for immediate access – but in far too many cases vehicle access has taken precedence over conservation, and intrusive parking has destroyed the intimate nature of the narrow streets. In some cases the lanes are used as rat runs, endangering any pedestrian who might wander down them.

There are other concerns. Ugly, intrusive road signs disfigure entrances, and all too frequently black tarmac patches mark where the lanes have been dug up for service access. Worst of all, large housing developments in once historic gardens have meant that the flint walls have been breached and high buildings, considered by many to be very insensitive to the surroundings, now tower above them.

The Friends of Lewes therefore considered that it was time for another book about the twittens to be published. This book is not a revision of Houghton's work. I felt that a more detailed look at the way the twittens developed and changed over the centuries would have wider interest, and I wanted to draw attention to those that are still peaceful and relatively unspoilt – almost entirely narrow paths without access for vehicles.

Houghton defined a twitten as a lane that runs at right angles to the principal highway. Most of those running south from the

High Street do indeed conform to this definition and date from Saxon times. However, Lewes is full of narrow paths, commonly called twittens, which are not straight and mostly of later date. Most of the lanes around the castle are like that, and they have their own chapter.

In the following pages we look at the history of both existing and conjectured twittens, and trace how they have evolved over the past twelve hundred years. Most importantly, we consider how modern development has affected the character of some of the most iconic twittens, assess the further threats that still exist and make suggestions to preserve and enhance what remains.

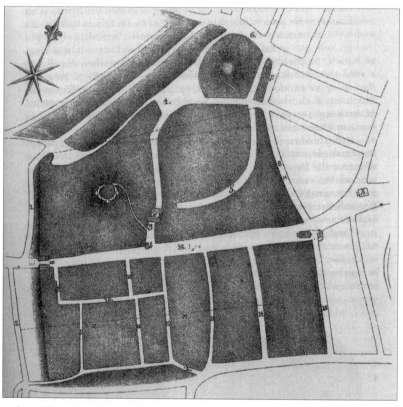

John Elliot's suggest Roman camp. (See facing page.)

Chapter One
What is a twitten?

The word 'twitten' was first recorded in the 13th century as 'twyten' and is found almost exclusively in south-east England, especially in Sussex. It relates to the early German word 'twiete', meaning a narrow lane or alleyway. The modern German word for between or amongst, 'zwischen', has the same root.

What were the origins of the twittens of Lewes? Early antiquarians believed that there had once been a large Romano-British town here that was later fortified by the Saxons and Normans. One, John Elliot, born in Lewes in 1725, went further: he hypothesised that the street plan of Lewes was based on the layout of a Roman legionary camp. His meticulously executed plan (*facing page*) showed the *via principia* on the line of the High Street between Westgate and Fisher Street. To the north lay the forum and *quaestorium* (the building of the supply officer), while the twittens to the south indicated the layout of a vast barracks for 12,000 men and 1800 horses. Sadly for Mr Elliot, relatively few Roman artefacts have been found in Lewes and modern archaeologists discount the possibility of any substantial Romano British settlement.

The first definite mention of Lewes in written documentation occurs in the Burghal Hideage, compiled in the reign of Edward the Elder (899–924), King of Wessex. This lists thirty-three fortified burhs in Wessex, of which Lewes was the eleventh largest.

Most of the lanes in Lewes commonly thought of as twittens run due south from the High Street. Those between St Nicholas Lane and Westgate almost certainly date from Saxon times, and the layout of the Saxon burh of Lewes was similar to that in other towns in the south-east. Regularly spaced side streets ran at right angles from a central spine road that extended from a west gate (more or less where the Norman gate was later built), to a probable east gate roughly on the site of the present war memorial. The building of the Norman castle meant that most of the Saxon street pattern north of the High Street would have been obliterated, although the present Fisher Street and Market Street may follow the original Saxon lanes. The distinctive street pattern remained virtually unchanged over the centuries and is clearly shown in William Figg's plan of 1799 (*pages 4–5*). At that time most of the gardens and fields bounded by the twittens were undeveloped, and the regular spacing between the twittens can be clearly seen.

John Houghton has argued that all the Lewes twittens were embodied in a 'grand design' using a plot width of about 20ft, each providing space for seven frontages to the High Street. His theory is based on a study of four hundred years of land tenure in Lewes and an examination of the widths of many of the present Georgian frontages. Almost all of these are multiples of 20ft, seeming to confirm his hypothesis. He believed that other medieval towns showed similar enduring plot patterns of possibly Saxon origin, and more recent work has supported this.

A number of archaeologists have examined the street plans of other Burghal Hidage towns. Biddle and Hill looked at seven towns and in each case found evidence of a Saxon street plan that definitely was not of Roman origin. They believed that all seven towns were originally fortified settlements, built in response to threats from Viking invaders. The settlement of the population within urban settlements with a regular street pattern was considered by them to be a deliberate policy undertaken in the reign of King Alfred, father of Edward the Elder. Other studies have suggested that a standard measurement, based on 16 pole units, could have been used in the layout of all Burghal Hidage towns.

Recently Mike Holmes decided to see if Lewes conformed to this hypotheses. Taking twelve west-east points from Westgate to

St Nicholas Lane, he measured the spacing between each. His measurement points included ten twittens (nine extant and one lost), the line of the medieval wall running from Westgate and the parish boundary between All Saints and St John sub Castro. He also included three north-south measuring points, the High Street, Stewards Inn Lane and Gatehouse Lane, a now lost back way. His results show a regularity of spacing that appears deliberate.

He considers that the street plan of Lewes was laid out on a grid of 64 poles in length, and linear features that may have been plot boundaries were spaced at four-pole intervals. His theory is based on a pole length of 18ft. Although a pole is generally taken to be 16½ft, measurements in the ninth century were not based on a centralised standard, and variation was therefore considerable. During the redevelopment of the Baxter's printworks site in St Nicholas Lane, an early medieval ditch was discovered and identified as a burh ditch, the first time such a feature has been recognised in Lewes. The line of this ditch probably represents the eastern boundary of the Saxon burh.

While the street layout of the area north of the High Street was almost entirely lost by the building of the Norman castle, it is possible to recognise the boundaries of the entire Saxon settlement by features such as the surviving medieval walls. There is also some evidence that between the river and the hill where the castle now stands there was a series of mounds, one of which was near the river crossing point at Malling.

Although the line of the burh ditch north of the castle has not been conclusively established, there is some archaeological evidence of a bank and ditch in the vicinity of Lancaster Street. The archaeologists differ about the date of these remains. While some think they could be Saxon, others suggest that King Stephen's reign is more likely. The probable line of the burh ditch is shown on page 14.

I have taken a broad approach to the streets included in this book. Some roads have sadly become major highways, but if there is evidence that they were once part of the ancient street pattern I have included them. I have also included notes on the lost twittens of Lewes, and these entries are shown in italics.

Chapter Two

The Saxon and Norman twittens south of the High Street

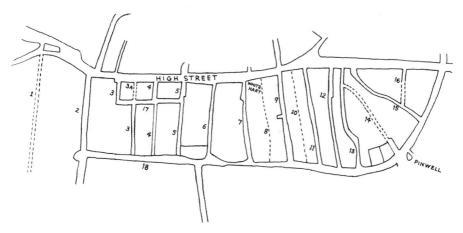

Existing and lost twittens south of the High Street. [Marietta Van Dyck]

Key:
1 Antioch Street; 2 Keere Street
3 Bull Lane (now includes Paines Twitten)
3a Former line of Bull Lane, lost by 1772
4 St Swithun's Lane; 5 St Martin's Lane
6 Watergate Lane; 7 St Andrew's Lane
8 Olde Scole Strete (lost); 9 St Mary's Lane (now Station Street)
10 Lost twitten on boundary between St Nicholas and
*   St Mary-in-Foro parishes*
11 St Nicholas Lane; 12 Walwers Lane; 13 Church Twitten
14 Pinwell Street (lost); 15 Brooman's Lane
16 Fullers Passage (largely lost)

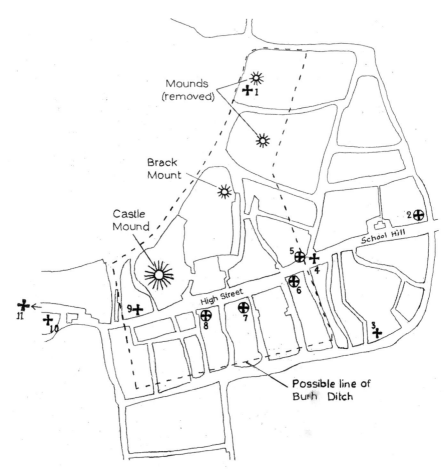

Churches, mounds and possible line of the burh ditch. [Marietta Van Dyck]

Key to churches:
1 St John; 2 Holy Trinity; 3 All Saints; 4 St Nicholas
5 St Peter the Less; 6 St Mary in Foro; 7 St Andrew; 8 St Martin
9 St Michael; 10 St Peter; 11 St Mary (later St Anne)

Of the twittens and lanes south of the High Street and School Hill, only those that lie within the burh can be considered to be definitely of Saxon origin. Those beyond the Westgate and (Saxon) Eastgate are much more likely to be medieval.

John Houghton has argued that frontage measurements indicate that the 'grand design' extended beyond the Saxon burh, possibly to include tenements that were built outside the walls, but this seems unlikely as there are considerable differences between the twittens definitely within the Saxon boundaries and those outside. The narrow streets within the burh run in a straight line, whereas the first twitten beyond the Eastgate is Walwers Lane, which has a definite kink to the south-east: the more easterly the street, the more pronounced the bend.

Hardly any of the Saxon names survive, but several recall the names of long lost churches. Ten churches are known to have existed in Lewes by 1121, not including those at Southover, Cliffe and Malling. Documentary evidence for those founded by the Saxons is missing, but certainly some were there before the Conquest, probably including the mother churches of St John's, St Michael's and All Saints. (Their position is shown on the facing page.) Many lanes have undergone several changes of identity over the centuries, but in this part of Lewes the basic medieval street pattern is little altered.

I decided that the most logical way to look at these twittens was to start in the west, just outside the Westgate and to work eastwards. I also decided to include a couple of lanes that run parallel to the High Street, since they are both part of the essential twitten network.

ANTIOCH STREET (mostly lost)

Now barely three car lengths long, Antioch Street was once a highway that ran from the crest of the town to Southover, where it linked with St. James' Street.

In 1559 the whole street was apparently destroyed by fire, and by 1595 'every trace of its buildings having disappeared', the land was enclosed – a fact confirmed by the historian and antiquarian John Rowe in 1622.

As late as 1861 (before Grange Road was constructed) the line of the old street was 'easily traced in a southerly direction through a large field in front of Southover Grange'. When the paddock opposite Southover Grange was levelled in 1957, to form a new playing field for the adjacent school, a well and some medieval pottery were found, and traces of the old road were revealed when the embankment on the south side of Grange Road was cut away.

It is possible that the name 'Antioch' was brought to Lewes by Crusaders returning after the capture of Antioch in south-east-Turkey in 1099. Antioch played an extremely important part in Christian history. It was the base for St Paul's journeys and the place where followers of Jesus were first called Christians.

It is more likely, however, that a community of Jewish immigrants may have been allowed to settle there. In Norman and Plantagenet times Jews were permitted to live only in isolated communities, usually outside the walls. Forbidden to undertake agricultural or craftwork, they were forced to limit their activities to money lending, purchasing tolerance and protection by submitting to heavy taxation by the realm.

KEERE STREET

Although this picturesque lane lies just outside the west gate of the Saxon burh, it is extremely likely that it existed before the Conquest. The name could derive from the old British word 'caer', which was applied to fortified places and, in this case, would mean the street in the fosse or ditch of the town wall.

Keere Street.

Alternatively the name may have originated from the Saxon word 'cerre' which means 'winding or sloping'.

The earliest reference to this street name appears in an ancient deed dated 1272, where it is referred to as 'the path called "Kerestrete"'. As with neighbouring Antioch Street, it is possible that immigrants fleeing from persecution in Europe could have settled here. Another theory on the origin of the street name suggests that the word 'kere' or 'keer' is a phonetic corruption of 'Cahors' – a word which appears at the time of the Norman Conquest and which was commonly descriptive of merchant foreigners who came to this country in the wake of the Norman invasion – diasporas that continued in later centuries as more fled from political strife and oppression. More recently, local historian John Bleach has suggested that the original name was Keyer Street, or street of the keymakers.

This is one of the most photographed streets in Lewes and, since parking and vehicle access are prohibited, it has largely retained its character. George IV, when Prince of Wales, was said to have driven a coach and four down the steep hill on his way from Lewes Races to be entertained by the Newton family who lived at Southover Grange. His progress must have been impeded by the cobblestones that still feature in the street today. Most Lewes streets were once paved with them, but sadly Keere Street is now the only one where they remain to any significant extent. The cobblestones were familiarly known as 'petrified kidneys' because of their blueish colour, but they have mostly disappeared, to be replaced by the more usual brown stones.

The brick pavements bordering the cobbles are wider than they used to be and, although rather uneven, are thankfully intact without the patches of black tarmac that disfigure many of the other twittens.

BULL LANE and PAINES TWITTEN

Bull Lane was probably the first of the Saxon streets that ran from the spine road down to the circuit of the Saxon wall. Originally it was a straight road running at right angles to the High Street down to the town wall above what is now Southover Road. Confusingly, the very short lane now known as Bull Lane was not part of the Saxon street. The original lane between High Street and Stewards Inn Road had been lost by 1772, when records note that it was 'now enclosed'. It was possibly realigned

Bull House. [Marietta Van Dyck]

to its present course so that it skirted a garden owned by a Mr Mitchell. The lower part continued to be known as Bull Lane until 1949, when it was renamed Paines Twitten.

Bull House, which retains many 15th and 16th century features, was in medieval times an inn called the Bull. It stood conveniently just inside the west gate and was frequented by travellers who used this entrance to the town. Sir Henry Goring bought the old inn in 1583. He built on the south side of it a large town house, the shell of which was extensively altered and converted in 1698 into the present Westgate Chapel. The Bull, it seems, had long since ceased to be used as a hostelry, although the name has survived the centuries.

The house became a lasting memorial by sheltering under its roof Thomas Paine, author of *Rights of Man* and champion of the American and French revolutions. He arrived in Lewes in 1768 to work as an excise officer, and lodged at Bull House, then a grocer's shop owned by Samuel Olive. After Olive's death he married his daughter Elizabeth, and ran the shop until April 1774, when he separated from his wife and shortly afterwards emigrated to America.

The house was bought and restored by John Every in 1922, and he presented it to the Sussex Archaeological Society, which still owns it. Although it is not open to the public on a regular basis, there are occasional open days as well as tours for pre-booked groups.

Paine's Twitten runs from Bull Lane almost to Southover Road.

ST SWITHUN'S LANE AND GREEN LANE

Like Bull Lane, the original Saxon lane has undergone many changes over the centuries. Nowadays only the very short connection from the High Street to Stewards Inn Lane is given the name St Swithun's Lane. It is not until 1624 that St Swithun's Lane, alias Stewards Inn Lane, appears in town records. The fine Georgian house now occupied by Lloyds Bank at 82 High Street, on the corner of St Swithun's Lane, used to be known as St Swithun's House.

St Swithun was a 9th century Bishop of Winchester, but dedications to the saint are uncommon. Indeed there is only one church (at East Grinstead) dedicated to him in all of Sussex, Surrey and Kent. However in the late 15th century there was a 'light' or illumination dedicated to St Swithun in St Michael's church nearby. It is probable that this actually meant there was an illuminated statue, or possibly painting, of the saint. It is conjectured that this statue may originally have been in a chapel attached to the Stewards Inn. (*See Steward's Inn Lane on page 24.*)

In 1799 William Figg marked St Swithun's Lane as continuing down the line of what is now known as Green Lane. This narrow lane runs from Stewards Inn Lane to Elm Grove, just above Southover Road. William Green had a garden there in the late 18th century and gave part of it to widen the adjoining St Martin's Lane. Shortly afterwards it became known as Green Lane. In 1906 the garden was sold for development and the present St Swithun's Terrace was built there.

Green Lane is only a footway, and therefore could be one of the most attractive of the twittens. The fine flint wall is ancient, but when St Swithun's Terrace was built the houses were given back entrances that opened onto Green Lane. Apart from the many breaches in the wall (the one in Paines Twitten was similarly abused), the tarmac surface of the lane is now in a poor condition.

ST. MARTIN'S LANE

The church of St. Martin stood near the lane which bears its name. Although documentary evidence is lacking, this may have been a flourishing church in Saxon Lewes. It has been suggested that the medieval stone vault which still exists beneath 72 High Street may have formed part of the vanished church. In the year 1337, John, Bishop of Chichester, issued a decree for the amalgamation of certain impoverished churches in Lewes, and the parish of St. Martin was absorbed into the parish of St. Andrew. Two centuries later, in 1545, St. Andrew was united with St. Michael.

Fifteenth century and later records quote an alternative name for the lane – Snellings Lane – so preserving the name of the family of Snellyng, the fishers, of whom the earliest mention appears to be in 1296. In 1564 a market house was built in the

Looking up St Martin's Lane. [Marietta Van Dyck]

High Street opposite this lane and in front of Castlegate. The cost was met by a legacy of £10 by Alice Holter, the widow of a high constable of the town, and £10 provided by the Fellowship of Twelve. In 1622 John Rowe described the Fellowship as follows: *'There is and hath been (time out of mind) within this Borough a society of the wealthier and discrete sort of the Townsmen commonly called the Twelve, out of which society the Constables are always chosen, the elder by course according to this seniority, the younger is chosen by the elder...'*

St Andrews Lane became known as Market Lane, a name it retained long after the market had moved in 1792, and causing great confusion with the similarly named street on the opposite side of the High Street.

There is only limited vehicle access to St Martin's Lane but, as the photograph shows, this docs not stop motorists trying to drive up it. In this case the driver told us that her satellite navigation directed her up the lane!

The Southover Street entrance would look better without parking bays, and the road surface is in very bad condition. Red brick pavements line part of the street, and the appearance of the lane would be vastly improved if resurfacing work were done in a red tarmac as in nearby Pipe Passage.

STEWARD'S INN LANE

Steward's Inn Lane is now a nondescript lane running parallel with the High Street between Bull Lane and St Martin's Lane. It once opened onto the High Street near the present St. Swithun's Lane. This was probably the entrance to the inn or precinct of the offices of the steward to the lords of the castle. Early deeds dating from 1309 refer to 'the house of Earl Warenne called La Perynne', which can be identified as being situated here, and which may have been the steward's residence.

The office of steward no doubt lost its importance in 1347 when the castle ceased to be the lord's residence on the death of the last of the de Warennes. The account of the income from the Duke of Norfolk's share of the barony of Lewes for the year 1498 reveals a state of disuse, as 'the Styward's Inn charged at 7d. raised nothing therefrom in this year', although the 'pigeonhouse in the Stywardsynne' brought in a rent of 3s. 4d. A disastrous fire in 1592 must have removed surviving traces of the steward's domain, and it probably existed in name only by 1620, when orders were given to dismantle much of the castle and its precincts to provide building material at 4d. a load.

ELM GROVE

This attractive pathway between the bottom of Keere Street and St Martin's Lane would once have been a walkway along the town wall, stretches of which can still be seen above and below it. At the time of writing the flint walls are being carefully repaired, an initiative which should be repeated in many other parts of the old town.

WATERGATE LANE

This would always have been a busy street, since the present Watergate Lane leads down to the site of the old water gate in the town wall. This was situated north of the mill pond, an extensive spread of water formed by the Winterbourne stream. A rental for the year 1498 includes a record of 'land lying to the east of the bridge of Watergate'.

The fine flint wall that surrounds Pelham House runs down the east side of Watergate Lane. Unfortunately this lane, along with St Andrews Lane and St Mary's Lane (Station Street) has become part of the traffic circulation system in the town centre. Parking is also allowed on part of the street. The ambience would be greatly improved if parking was prohibited and the road was surfaced with paviors similar to those laid in Market Street.

Watergate Lane.

ST. ANDREW'S LANE

When Henry VIII ordered the destruction of Lewes Priory in 1537, the church of St. Andrew lost its patron. After struggling along for a few years it was eventually closed down, and its parish was merged with that of St. Michael in 1545.

The actual site of St. Andrew's Church is not definitely known, but during drainage excavations in the courtyard of Pelham House in 1890, foundations were exposed which were thought to be the remains of the church.

St Andrew's Lane is narrower than Watergate Lane, and although south bound through traffic is allowed, it still retains much of its twitten like character. The high flint wall on the west side forms the boundary of the garden of Pelham House and is largely unbreached, with vegetation hanging down into the lane. This exceptional Elizabethan mansion, built in the 16th century by George Goring, is now a hotel. The date 1579 can be seen inside.

Pelham House.

The Gorings were a powerful family in the reign of Elizabeth, and a later George Goring was the commander of the royalist forces of Charles 1. He was captured by the parliamentarians and sentenced to death, but reprieved and forced to sell his estates. The house was bought by Thomas Pelham, whose descendent Thomas Holles Pelham became Duke of Newcastle and first lord of the treasury (prime minister) in 1758. Visitors having a drink or tea at the hotel can wander around the garden, the only one left in the twittens with access for the public.

The twitten would be enormously improved if the tarmac were replaced by paviors.

OLDE SCOLE STRETE (lost)
The entrance to the car park of the White Hart Hotel is all that remains of this lost twitten that is known to have descended from the 'east end of the White Hart Inn to the South Rampart', coinciding with the parish boundary between St Andrew's and St Mary-in-Foro. It was recorded as Olde Scole Strete in 1316, and possibly Tollers Lane in 1511.

STATION STREET (ST MARY'S LANE)
Of all the twittens in Lewes, the former St Mary's Lane (and colloquially known as Simmery Lane) is the one that has been most degraded. It is one of the busiest streets in Lewes, carrying all northbound traffic from Southover and Lewes station. The pavements are narrow, and since there are traffic lights at the junction with the High Street, air quality is poor.

The lane was originally named after the church of St. Mary-in-Foro (in the market) which stood on the site of the old shop at High Street corner. Its parish was merged with St. John-sub-Castro in 1538 and the church was converted into a parsonage, passing later to a more secular use. The cellar and structure of the present shop, now Flint, still retain traces of the old church.

In 1857, a new passenger railway station was built on its present site, replacing the original station in Friars Walk, and in its honour the approach road from the town centre was renamed Station Street. There was strong opposition to changing the old style of St. Mary's Lane, and it became the scene of 'The battle of the boards', with the old and new name-plates being substituted almost daily by the opposing parties. Eventually the 'progressives' won, although for a long time both name-plates were exhibited one above the other at the top of the street. The long history of Station Street is described on a display board that has recently been erected halfway down the street.

LANE RUNNING FROM 44/45 HIGH STREET (lost)
The parish boundary of All Saints and St John-sub-Castro runs southward in a line between nos. 44 and 45 High Street. This would once have been the boundary between St Nicholas and St Mary-in-Foro parishes. Both Houghton and Holmes suggest that if the Anglo-Saxon street layout conformed to a regular pattern based on multiples of four poles, there would have been a plot boundary on this line. No trace of this lost twitten remains, and there is no documentary evidence that it existed.

ST. NICHOLAS LANE
Excavations before redevelopment in St Nicholas Lane (the Printworks) have recently revealed an early medieval ditch which has been interpreted as a burh ditch. This almost certainly shows the eastern boundary of the Anglo Saxon settlement. The excavations also produced many finds from the 9th to 11th centuries, including a coin hoard dating from the reign of Edward the Elder (899–924).

If the identification of the burh ditch is correct, then St Nicholas Lane would be the last of the Saxon twittens on the south side of the High Street. The lanes further to the east are much less straight and have a definite medieval character.

In the 14th century the plague Black Death decimated the population of England. The social upheavals of those times resulted in the impoverished parish of St. Nicholas being united with All Saints, and the little church of St. Nicholas, which stood at the top of School Hill roughly where the war memorial now stands, was left to decay. Its tower, however, survived, and became known as the Broken Church. In the bell loft was hung the great town bell Gabriel, which was 'new cast in 1555' and which used to ring the curfew.

In 1761 the remains of the broken church were pulled down. The stones were used to fill in the town well, which was in the middle of the roadway opposite the Crown Inn and had become an obstruction to traffic. The bell Gabriel was stored for thirty years until 1792, when it was re-hung in the newly built Market Tower – where it remains today In November 1934, workmen laying a water main in the road opposite 39 and 40 High Street uncovered skeletons which were probably the remains of burials at the old church.

Unfortunately St Nicholas Lane is another twitten that has lost much of its character. This is not a recent phenomenon. One of the most important industries in the history of Lewes was founded here, and the site remained in industrial use until the residential development that was completed in 2010.

John Baxter came to Lewes in 1802 and founded the printing works that continued in this lane until recently. (It was his son George who made the name famous: he invented a process of printing in colour: until then there had been hand colouring.) A disastrous fire in 1952 destroyed most of the 19th century plant, and the rebuilding proved to be as nondescript as most architecture of the period. The recent redevelopment was a chance to restore some of the integrity of the twitten. Although there was considerable controversy over the design of the new homes and small workshops, most would agree that the buildings are a great improvement on what was there.

The road has only two spaces for cars, and it is therefore particularly unfortunate that the ambience has been largely destroyed by the ugly double yellow lines on both sides of the narrow lane. (*Photograph below.*) These are quite unnecessary – simple signs would have been sufficient. New guidelines to reduce the impact of road markings and signs have recently been issued, and it is hoped that East Sussex County Council will take note and remove the yellow lines here and in other twittens similarly disfigured.

Looking up St Nicholas Lane to the High Street.

WALWERS LANE

Walwers Lane lies just below the site of the Saxon Eastgate and as such is likely to be of medieval origin. The development on the Baxter's site has also affected Walwers Lane, but this narrow pedestrian route has also suffered substantial redevelopment on the east side. Until comparatively recently this second site

Walwer's Lane

was part of the garden of School Hill House. Although a small area of garden remains, in the 1960s the county council erected 'temporary' prefabricated offices for use by the education department. More recently these buildings were used by Lewes District Council. It was considered necessary to lower the wall in front of the building so that those walking along the twitten could get a really good view of the prefab.

There were no tears, then, when it was pulled down, but the Friends of Lewes asked for the wall to be rebuilt to its original height as part of the redevelopment. This was not done, so a chance of restoring some of the character of this lane was lost. Even so, Walwers Lane remains one of the most rewarding of the twittens to stroll along.

Walwers Lane perpetuates the memory of William le Walewere, who was one of the members of parliament for Lewes in 1319 and 1323–4, and who once lived there. His name appears as a taxpayer in a subsidy roll of 1296, as also does Matilda Walwer, a widow, who was probably his mother. In Victorian times the lane became known as Birdcage Lane, as a result of the ornithological pursuits of John Maxfield Smith (high constable in 1879), who lived at School Hill House in the latter part of the last century. His collection of 175 showcases of birds was preserved for many years in the former borough museum in Albion Street (later the library, but now offices), and was later moved to the Booth Museum in Brighton.

CHURCH TWITTEN
Church Twitten runs from the High Street to All Saints Church, now owned by Lewes Town Council and used as a community and arts centre. It is rather sad that the only lanes that actually have twitten in their name have all been renamed in the 20th century. In the case of Church Twitten the name was changed from Church Lane in 1954 to avoid confusion with Church Lane

in South Malling, which became a main road serving the large estate being built around it. To add to the confusion, there is another Church Lane beyond Westgate, between St Anne's Church and Rotten Row

The name-change never affected the character of this most iconic of Lewes's twittens. Bounded on the right by the garden of School Hill House and on the left by that of Lewes House (*below*), the high flint walls were (and still are) overhung by the leaves of plane and lime trees. The kink in the lane about half way down adds to its attractiveness.

The walls were virtually unbreached save for a small opening on the left where a stone gateway allowed entrance into the School Hill house garden. While much of the garden of Lewes House remained intact, a 'temporary' building was erected forty years ago at the lower end. The remaining part of the old orchard was used for staff parking by Lewes District Council, who own Lewes House.

The garden of Lewes House.

A few years ago the council decided to sell the entire lower garden for development, along with the garden of School Hill House. To link the two parts of the development it was thought necessary to demolish part of the flint wall in a section that had remained intact over the centuries. The wall was to be rebuilt after construction finished, but new gateways would be made on both sides of the twitten.

There was enormous opposition to this proposal, but it went ahead. It is a relief, therefore, to report that great care (and expense) was taken with the work. On the School Hill House side the new stone gateway (*below*) successfully copies the centuries-old gate further up the lane. The opposite gateway into the Lewes House site is also very well done. However, at the time of writing, only the School Hill House part of the development has been completed. In the Lewes House garden the buildings have been demolished but rebuilding has been delayed.

The new gateway.

Many of the trees that overhang the twitten are covered by preservation orders, and will therefore remain, but other features of the garden that had somehow survived among the parking bays have been destroyed.

Because Church Twitten is entirely pedestrian, unlike other twittens, it will not be disfigured by parking, but we have to hope that the completed development will not dominate too much.

Church Twitten, with its kink.

PINWELL STREET *(lost)*

Pinwell Street led originally from near School Hill down to the ancient Pinwell which once belonged to the Cluniacs. It was first recorded in 1280. The Pinwell was a powerful source of fresh water for the townsfolk and the spring appears to have been supplemented by water channelled from the wetland into a town ditch. In 1244 the Franciscans constructed a vault over the ditch and included it in their new monastery precinct.

Although legends suggest that the name comes from a superstition that evil spirits could be placated if a pin was cast into the well, it is more likely that it was called after the owner of a house on the site. The 14th century record of bequests to Lewes Priory includes the gift by Agnes-de-Pinwell of a house in Pinwell Street

The Pinwell remained in use for many centuries. Eventually the approach to the well was deemed unsafe: it was sealed in 1838 and replaced by a pump at the expense of John Hoper, a local solicitor. In 1874, the constables of the borough removed the pump, enclosed the ground and erected a drinking fountain against the churchyard wall, the water supply being taken

The Pinwell drinking fountain in Friars Walk.
[Marietta Van Dyck]

from the public main. The fountain was restored in 1888 but in the 1930s, after it fell into disuse, the water supply was cut off and it became derelict. A number of years ago the Friends of Lewes restored the exterior to its 19th century appearance.

BROOMAN'S LANE

This most easterly of the surviving twittens, like its former neighbour, the lost Pinwell Street, runs in a south-easterly direction. It may have the longest recorded history of any of the Lewes twittens, probably having originally been the long-lost Plantagenet Street which once existed in Lewes. Hameline, bastard brother of Henry II, the first of the Plantagenet line of English kings, became the fifth Lord of Lewes in 1164. The emblem of the family was a sprig of broom (the *planta genista*, from which their surname derives). The association of the names Plantagenet and Brooman is unlikely to be coincidence.

The lane appears in early 14th century records, when John Rygate of Lewes, a member of a brotherhood of archers known as the Gild of St. Sebastian, bequeathed to the brotherhood a house in Broomeman Street. About the year 1600 the lane was described as 'Broomemanstreet, lying on the west side of the almshouses on Schoole Hill and bending down towards the friars wall'. An ancient house for the reception of paupers once stood at the corner of this lane on the site now occupied by 31 High Street. By the mid 18th century the property had become dilapidated, and in 1758 it was decided to sell it and build new almshouses in St. Nicholas Lane. The old almshouses appear, however, to have survived until well into the 19th century, when they were replaced by shop premises which survive to this day.

The northern part of the lane, which is pedestrianised, is extremely attractive. The high walls that border the Lewes House gardens are unbreached, and development on the left-hand side is limited. Further along there was a substantial amount of development in the 1980s, and considerable care was taken over the design and the use of high quality materials. No vehicle access was allowed and, by and large, the lane remained unspoilt. What a pity then that about twenty years later the same care was not taken when the large building now used by

Fuller's Passage, looking towards School Hill.

the East Sussex Downs and Weald Primary Care Trust was erected. The building fronts Friars Walk and in itself is a reasonable example of modern design, but sadly a large private car park was allowed behind it. Access is from Brooman's Lane, and the car park is extremely visible since the wall is much lower than in the rest of the lane. Above the car park the wall has been built to nearly its original height. The materials are flint with bands of brick which would have been acceptable, but most unfortunately the bricks chosen are of a harsh red, quite out of keeping in a conservation area. Even after ten or more years there is no sign of any toning down in colour. Similar bricks, regrettably, have been used in many other parts of the conservation area.

Steamer Trading, the kitchen equipment shop on School Hill, owns the large vacant plot behind their premises that opens onto Brooman's Lane. They have permission to build four houses there, and we have to hope that the inclusion of Lewes in the national park will mean that more care is taken with design and detailing than has been the case so far.

FULLER'S PASSAGE (mostly lost)
Fuller's Passage is today only a short cul-de-sac, but William Figg's map of Lewes drawn in 1799 shows that the lane once continued and joined Brooman's Lane about halfway down. Fuller's Passage is opposite the conjectured site of Holy Trinity Church, which was lost in the 13th century. John Houghton considered that the standard pattern of the frontages of the Saxon burh continued down School Hill and indicated a 'lost twitten' above the frontages of 11–19 High Street, just below the entrance to Fuller's Passage.

The recent discovery of the burh ditch in St Nicholas Lane (if confirmed) makes it unlikely that this was a Saxon twitten, but it is almost certainly of medieval origin. The present name probably derives from Thomas Trayton Fuller, a Whig MP who lived in one of the large Georgian houses opposite. Ancient cellars and a (now blocked) passage in the vicinity probably predate the existing buildings. Fuller was, and is, a common name in Lewes. William Fuller, a draper, owned 18 and 19 High Street, and the name could also derive from him.

The first part of Fuller's Passage contains some attractive buildings. It would be easy to enhance this area, but unhappily it then opens into a parking area which is very scruffy. The entrance to the medieval passage is easily visible, but on the day of my visit was filled with rubbish. Behind the car park is the large vacant plot mentioned in the previous entry. A revised planning application is shortly to be submitted. It is understood that this will include rejoining Fullers Passage to Brooman's Lane. If the work is done with the care it deserves, it should mean that this lost twitten is once again a vibrant part of the fabric of Lewes.

Chapter Three

The northern 'twittens' and the castle

It is virtually certain that the regular street pattern of the Saxon burh extended north of the spine road. Almost all these streets were obliterated when William de Warenne started to build his castle after the Conquest. Although many excavations have been undertaken in different parts of the town the northern boundaries of Saxon Lewes have not been not conclusively

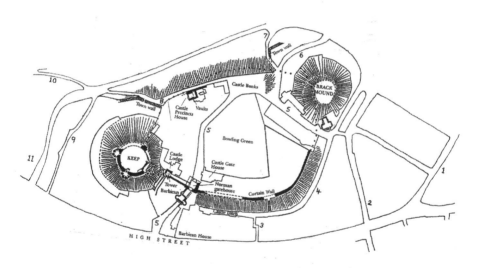

The lanes and paths around the castle. [Marietta Van Dyck]

Key:
1 Market Street
2 Fisher Street
3 Pope's Passage
4 Castle Ditch Lane
5 Castle Gate

6 Castle Banks
7 Castle Rise
8 Castle Lane
9 Pipe Passage
10 Paddock Twitten
11 Westgate Street

established. There is agreement, however, that the western boundary of the Norman castle precinct follows the line of the Saxon ramparts.

David Hill, an authority on Saxon burhs, has suggested that the ditch might then have run roughly along the line of West Street and Market Street to the east gate. However this would mean that St John's church lay outside the burh. Although it is possible that St John's actually predates the burh (it is built on a fortified position that may be of pagan origin) it is very unlikely that it lay outside it. Undoubtedly one of the richest churches in Saxon Lewes, it is mentioned several times in the Domesday book. It was also the church in which Magnus, Prince of Denmark, ended his days as an anchorite.

Although St John's church was largely rebuilt in Victorian times, a coffin said to be Magnus's can still be seen, built into the wall of the church. The Latin inscription remembers Magnus, but the coffin is now known to date from the 12th century. The identity of Magnus remains a mystery. Early historians suggested that he was a son of King Harold of England, with one actually believing that he was Harold himself, who escaped from the Battle of Hastings, wounded but alive, and took sanctuary in the church!

Other findings support the premise that the burh extended as far as the river. John Bleach has found evidence of a series of mounds sloping down to a river crossing that links to the Roman road that can still be made out below Malling Down. The two most northerly survive as Brack Mount and Castle Mount, the twin mottes of the Norman castle. Possibly the burh ditch then followed the line of North Street and Market Street up to the east gate.

What evidence is there of these missing northern twittens? William Figg's map (*pages 4–5*) shows a grid of pastures between North Street and St John's church. In 1257 the now lost Lodders Street led from Fisher Street to the south-east corner of

St John's camp (St John-sub-Castro is the full name of the church). The line of the lane later became the boundary between St John's Croft and Pelham Field. It is conjecture that this grid layout predates the Conquest, but it seems very likely that Fisher Street and Market Street were part of Saxon Lewes.

Some of the most attractive lanes in Lewes are found in the environs of the castle, and they deserve inclusion in this book even if they do not strictly conform to the definition of a twitten. I have also included the two major highways of Market Street and Fisher Street because of their historical significance. Entries in this section run from east to west, with a bit of juggling to accommodate the winding lanes in Castle Precincts.

MARKET STREET

Market Street is now one of the busiest streets in Lewes. Pay a visit after 10pm or in the small hours of the morning and you might then think what an attractive street it is, with its red brick

Market Street. [Marietta Van Dyck]

pavements and paved carriageway – the result of a recent county council make-over. Unfortunately at all other times the volume of heavy traffic makes contemplation of this interesting street virtually impossible, and the foundations of the newly paved carriageway are collapsing under the weight of traffic.

While Market Street and its extension, North Street, are of undoubted early origin, there seem to be few records until Tudor times. A local resident, John Aylard, who died in 1544, gave his name to the lane, but in 1792 a new market was built to replace one opposite Castle Gate and the ancient bell Gabriel was rehung in the new market tower. It is still there today, and the market hall has a new lease of life with a flourishing local produce market every Friday.

FISHER STREET
Fisher Street is opposite St Mary's Lane and runs in a straight line from the High Street. to West Street. Records date from the 13th century when the lost lane, Loddere Street, is known to have run from Fisher Street to St John's churchyard. It may have taken its name from a fish market held there. For centuries, the fishwives, known as Juggs, brought their fish by pack donkeys over the downs from Brighthelmstone (Brighton) to sell in Lewes.

Fisher Street is far too narrow for the amount of traffic that uses it. Air quality measurements are the worst in Lewes, and unlike Market Street, there has been no attempt to improve the ambience of the street. It is a sad fate for a street that has existed for over a thousand years.

POPE'S PASSAGE
Popes Passage is a narrow footway that leads from the High Street to Castle Ditch Lane, site of the dry moat of the castle. There is no evidence that Pope's Passage is of great antiquity. On Figg's map it appears as a narrow cul-de-sac, probably leading

to the stables of the Rainbow Inn (later rebuilt and recently renamed Lincolns). It is a useful cut through, but is not particularly attractive, passing as it does by the kitchens and dustbins of the public house. Like all Lewes passages, it may once have been part of the 'grand design', but the frontages were so disturbed by the building of the castle it is impossible to draw any conclusions.

CASTLE DITCH LANE

Castle Ditch Lane is now a cul-de-sac that branches from Mount Place, just opposite the very popular Lewes Arms Inn. The bailey of the castle was surrounded by a high bank, topped by a wall, still visible in places. Below the bank there was a dry moat, or ditch, and Castle Ditch Lane follows the line of this ditch.

Until recently the lane gave access to a number of small workshops, mostly built into the bank side. Most of these have now been extended and converted into housing. No. 18 is of special interest, since a fine Tudor stone door and window survives in the fabric of the building, used until very recently as a store. Marietta Van Dyck has made a delightful drawing of the arch (*below*). Apart from this, the buildings in the lane are undistinguished, and the south side of the lane gives access to the rear of the law courts and the former Beards Brewery.

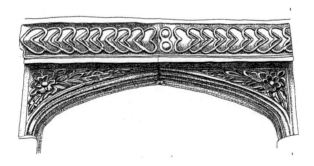

The Magic Circle, before (top) and today.

There is however one feature of real interest in the lane. A flight of steps leads along a path to the Magic Circle, once a hidden garden with stone seats surrounding a circular lily pond. It was built some years before the First World War by Frank Frankfort Moore, an Irish author who lived for many years at Castlegate House. He was a prolific writer (although surviving examples of his prose make it clear why he is now quite forgotten) and he told the story of his creation in *A Garden of Peace*, published in 1920 and in which Lewes is given the name Yardley Parva.

He spent a great deal of time redesigning the large garden of Castlegate House and brought in tons of rock, including monoliths from the Giants Causeway in Ireland. Somewhere he discovered an elaborate gateway with a peacock architrave and stone seats with an Egyptian motive. The circle survives, although the lily pond is long gone and the recent photo (*facing page, below*) shows the sorry state of the Magic Circle today. Now mainly used as a cut through to the adjacent car park, it still shows vestiges of its former glory and also gives access to a secluded grassy area under the curtain wall of the castle. It is hoped that the Friends of Lewes will be able to undertake a restoration project here. If permission is given by the owners, the county council, the Magic Circle will again be a quiet oasis right in the centre of Lewes, ideal for a relaxing sandwich break or a picnic spot for a family exploring the castle and town.

CASTLE GATE

Castle Gate leads from the High Street through to the bailey of the castle. Lewes castle has two mottes, both probably based on earlier fortified mounds, and the first keep of the castle may have been a wooden building on Brack Mount, the more northerly of the two. It may not have been until the 1090s that the bailey was extended, the second motte enlarged and the existing flint keep built on it.

The first building you see on your right is Barbican House, a first-rate Georgian building which is the headquarters of the Sussex Archaeological Society (SAS). The museum here should certainly be visited. Access to the castle keep is by a gate opposite Barbican House.

The perimeter wall of the bailey and castle was completed by about 1100. The monumental gatehouse has two arches with quoins of Caen stone. It is now used to store documents owned by the SAS. Passing through the gateway you come to two fine houses. That on the left, Castle Lodge, contains cellars that may have been part of the domestic buildings of the Norman castle but its more recent history is especially interesting. In 1904 it was bought by Charles Dawson, an amateur archaeologist and Uckfield solicitor who was a prominent member of the SAS. The Society was under the impression that he was buying the

Castle Gate. [Marietta Van Dyck]

house on their behalf, but they were sadly in error. They were furious and never forgave Dawson for his underhand behaviour.

Dawson took possession of Castle Lodge and lived there during the years he excavated a site at Piltdown, near Uckfield. There he 'found' a jaw and a skull that he claimed proved the link between ape and man. He received enormous acclaim for his discovery but in 1916 died suddenly (and in mysterious circumstances) before he could be awarded the FRS he so coveted. Many years later, in 1953, the jaw and skull of 'Piltdown Man' were found to be a forgery. Although it has never been proved that Dawson himself was responsible, it is known that he spent a great deal of time working alone in the cellars of Castle Lodge, so draw your own conclusions.

Castlegate House, opposite, is Georgian and was used for many years as a baby clinic by East Sussex County Council – generations of Lewesians received their free orange juice there. It has now returned to residential use. Next to it is the bowling green, once used as a tilting ground by de Warenne's knights. Unlike most bowling greens the surface is uneven, but it is still used regularly. The surrounding wall has been restored by the Friends of Lewes.

Although Castle Gate gives access to a car park used by the district council, bollards near the Maltings stops through traffic. The Maltings was once part of Beards brewery, but is currently used as East Sussex County Records Office. Unfortunately the Record Office is to be moved and the future of the Maltings is uncertain. Opposite there is a splendid view towards the site of the Battle of Lewes. An interpretation board allows the visitor to follow the course of the battle, but it was sadly defaced when I last visited. Hopefully a new board will be provided in time for the 750th anniversary of the Battle of Lewes in 2014.

Castle Gate has been well maintained and it is disappointing that its extension, leading down to Mount Place and the Lewes Arms pub, is very scruffy. The patched tarmac pavements cannot take away from the attractive views of Brack Mount and Brack Mount House, but this part of town deserves better maintenance.

CASTLE BANKS

This pretty lane winds down from Castle Gate to Mount Pleasant. No parking is allowed and the red brick pavements enhance the street. Brack Mount is owned by the Sussex Archaeological Society, but several lucky householders here have access to it. Although this is now an extremely desirable place to live, until the middle of the 20th century it was very run down, and some pretty houses were demolished in the name of 'slum clearance' as recently as 1960. The area may have been affected by the presence of the Poor House, predecessor of the workhouse built in the Wallands area in the mid 19th century.

The next four entries in this chapter are all footways, and although most do not conform to John Houghton's definition of a twitten as a lane running at right angles to a principal highway, they certainly fit the less rigorous description of a narrow footway.

CASTLE RISE

From the viewpoint in Castle Gate you can walk down a short flight of steps to Castle Rise, a short path that runs steeply down the castle bank to New Road. New Road itself dates from 1790, when Lewes started to expand beyond the boundaries of the medieval town, but before that it was a bridleway leading from Westgate Street to St John's and the river. Like so many of the twittens, Castle Rise is disfigured by ugly black patched tarmac. It urgently needs resurfacing.

Castle Banks. [Marietta Van Dyck]

CASTLE LANE

Castle Lane is one of the most appealing lanes in Lewes and its atmosphere is captured in a series of enchanting paintings by Peter Messer. (*See below.*) It runs along the castle bank below the garden of Castle Precincts House. This 18th century house stands on the site of many of the domestic buildings of the castle – probably including the hall, solar, chapel and kitchens – and, as with Castle Lodge, the cellars of the present house incorporate elements of the Norman buildings.

As late as 1775, an etching by James Lambert shows the high jagged curtain walls of the castle rising above the bank. Much of this wall is incorporated in the boundary wall of Castle Precincts House above the lane.

'October Evening, Castle Lane' by Peter Messer.

PIPE PASSAGE

Castle Lane runs along the bank until it reaches the start of New Road. At this point a flight of steps leads into Pipe Passage, a perfect footway which fits all definitions of 'twitten'. A new house has been built at the side of the steps. Great care has been taken with the design and materials used, and unlike so much modern infill in the centre, this cottage (*right*) actually enhances its delightful setting.

Pipe Passage gets its name from the pipe kiln that existed in the lane in the 18th and early 19th century. The remains can still be made out in a small area of neglected garden above Westgate Street. However, Pipe Passage itself is ancient, and was probably the sentry walk along the wall of the castle.

There are fine views of the castle and, unlike almost all other twittens in Lewes, great care has been taken over the resurfacing done in 2011. A narrow red brick pavement runs along part of the lane, and red tarmac has been chosen for resurfacing the pathway with, in my view, very successful results.

Pipe Passage was also the site of a windmill built in 1802, the base of which still stands, converted into a house. It was supposed to have been erected on Brack Mount, but the owner, the Duke of Norfolk, refused permission. Pipe Passage was

chosen instead, but the position was not successful and the mill closed in 1819. The Duke of Norfolk was, and is, one of the three lords of Lewes who once owned most of the town. They still own patches of manorial waste and unfortunately can be unenthusiastic about enhancement projects in the town. (*See next entry*)

The windmill, now known as 'The Round House', was bought by writers Virginia and Leonard Woolf in 1919. A plaque on the side of the house records her diary entry: '*We've bought a house in Lewes, on the spur of the*

The Round House.

moment. It's the butt end of an old windmill, so that all the rooms are either completely round or semi-circular.' Sad to say, Virginia's enthusiasm quickly waned and the Woolfs never lived there, preferring instead the much larger and more rural Monk's House in Rodmell.

The only disappointing note in Pipe Passage is the battered chain link fence that encloses the small patch of garden on the pipe factory site. It is to be hoped that this will soon be replaced by something more appropriate.

Pipe Passage, looking towards the Round House.

PADDOCK TWITTEN

This lane runs from Westgate Street down to Paddock Lane. Its age is unknown although there is some evidence that the tenement boundaries beyond Westgate conformed to the regular pattern found elsewhere. Certainly by 1624 the plots on the north side of St Anne's Hill were at least 250 feet deep, abutting a high bank above Paddock Lane. Paddock Twitten (an unofficial name) runs at a 45 degree angle down this bank.

In 2009 the Friends of Lewes wished to improve the lane by tidying the vegetation on the bank and repairing the low flint retaining wall. The town council offered to help fund the work. The bank had been fenced untidily, by the developer of a site in Westgate Street who was not, in fact, the owner of the land, which was manorial waste and so the joint property of the three lords of Lewes – the Marquis of Abergavenny (Nevill family), Earl De La Warr (Sackville family) and the Duke of Norfolk (Howard family).

The two latter lordships proved to have no interest in any of their Lewes manorial waste, but Lord Abergavenny accepted that the land in question was partly his responsibility. (The Nevills have a 50 per cent share in the lordship and the others 25 per cent each.) Alas, because of the dispute between the Nevill Estate and the developer, neither was prepared to assist the project. With ownership in dispute, it was reluctantly decided to abandon it. A pity, because this shaded walk is very pleasant, and much could have been done to enhance the area.

Facing page: Paddock Lane in Peter Messer's painting 'Leaf Man'.

WESTGATE STREET

The final entry in this section also lay outside the Saxon burh. Unlike the other streets discussed, it would have been little affected by the building of the Norman castle. Above Westgate Street looms the rampart that protected the Saxon town, later incorporated into the castle wall. The west gate of the burh was replaced on the same site in the 14th century. Vestiges of this gate survived until 1777 and remnants still remain in the foundations of buildings on either side of the High Street.

Westgate Street is now essentially a car park. It may, in common with Keere Street and Antioch Street, have originally housed immigrants who were not welcome within the burh. Much later, in Tudor times, it became known as Cutlers Bar because of the cutler trade carried out there. By the 19th century small houses backed right onto the wall, and in 1939 they were demolished as part of a slum clearance scheme. Only the 18th century sign of the White Lion Inn survives.

The sign of the White Lion.

An inn of this name is known to have existed in 1526 on School Hill, and the white lion is heraldic in origin, thought to have been the armorial bearing of Simon de Montfort. The sign is made of sheet copper and is gilded. Restoration, funded by the Friends of Lewes and Lewes Town Council, is expected shortly.

Westgate Street bears no sign of its origin as a twitten, if indeed it was ever one. Parking is so scarce in Lewes that the idea of redeveloping a town centre parking area is heresy, but the townscape would be greatly improved if small terraced houses (or flats with the appearance of houses) were rebuilt under the wall. Even better, the sign of the White Lion could be rehung outside a new hostelry in the street!

Postscript

It was suggested to me that this book should take the form of a walk around the twittens. Initially I thought this was a good idea, but when I worked on a route I soon realised that so many of them had been degraded that it was virtually impossible to make a continuous walk. Trying to write the history of the twittens seemed a better idea.

Of course walking around many of them is still a pleasure. I suggest starting at Castle Gate, walking through the Barbican and past the bowling green, pausing under the lime trees to look towards the battlefield. Then wander down Castle Lane to Pipe Passage, before crossing the road and tackling Keere Street. Follow Elm Grove, and then go up Paine's Twitten or Green Lane. After that it gets more difficult. You could go down St Martin's Lane and back up St Andrew's Lane, but then you probably should skip ahead to Walwers Lane, even though it has been seriously affected by development. Much more hopeful is the iconic Church Twitten, while the northern two-thirds of Broomans Lane makes you very angry to see what has happened at the bottom!

What of the future? Any further access for vehicles must be resisted, and removing all but the most essential parking from all the historic twittens should be a priority. But probably most important of all is attention to detail. It is often not development in itself that is so disastrous, but the slovenly way in which materials are selected and the creation of incongruous roof lines and perspectives. Then there is the bureaucratic use of traffic signage, and the heavy application of the dreaded yellow lines.

All these are unnecessary, and conservation societies such as the Friends of Lewes do their utmost to see that standards are maintained. Far too often their comments on a development are ignored, although to be fair to Lewes District Council, recent developments in the historic core do seem to have been to a higher standard. We await the completion of the Lewes House development with trepidation but some optimism.

In recent years maintenance of the pedestrian twittens in particular has been very poor. An exception is Pipe Passage, and this does show how easy it is to enhance a small street by a judicious choice of materials. On a much larger scale, Market Street was successfully repaved. Using similar materials in the other throughways such as Watergate Lane, St Andrews Street, Station Street and Fisher Street would make a huge difference to the townscape.

Finally it behoves us all to be vigilant. When development becomes necessary (and it is inevitable that some will occur), look at the plans and make constructive suggestions. There are far too many individuals and organisations in Lewes whose input is limited to dismissing everything or proposing wildly uneconomic or inappropriate solutions. Lewes is now in the South Downs National Park. Sensible comment will be welcomed and we should work with the Park authority and Lewes District Council to make the very best of our town.

Bibliography

Biddle, M. and Hill, D. 1971 'Late Saxon Planned Towns', *Antiquaries Journal 51*, 70–85

Brent, Colin 2004 *Pre-Georgian Lewes*

Davy, L.S. and Clark, K. 2010 *The Street Names of Lewes*

Holmes, Michael 2010 'The street plan of Lewes and the Burghal Hidage', *SAC* 148*, 71–78

Horsfield, T.J. 1827 *The History and Antiquities of Lewes and its Vicinity*

Houghton, John 1991 *Lewes Twittens*

Houghton, John 1986 'Burgage tenure and topography in Lewes', *SAC 124*, 119–28

Moore, F. Frankfort 1920 *A Garden of Peace*

* *Sussex Archaeological Collections*